Successful Living
30 Powerful Biblical Truths
(1-5)

Volume 1 of 6

Marco A. Martinez

THESE VOLUMES OF POWERFUL BIBLICAL TRUTHS
FOR SUCCESSFUL LIVING ARE PRESENTED TO YOU BY:

Marco A. Martinez, President
Best Friends Consulting, Inc.
www.BestFriendsConsulting.com

Marco A. Martinez, Consultant
Marco@30biblicaltruths.com

Copyright © 2013. All rights reserved. No part of this book may be reproduced by any means without written permission from Best Friends Consulting, except in the case of brief quotations within critical articles and reviews.

Scripture quotations not otherwise marked are from the New International Version © 2010 by International Bible Society.

Best Friends Consulting, Inc.
2nd Edition December 2013

ISBN: 149231465X
ISBN-13: 978-1492314653

Cover artwork by Skillful Antics - www.skillfulantics.com

Successful Living
30 Powerful Biblical Truths
(1-5)

Volume 1 of 6

Marco A. Martinez

DEDICATION

This book is dedicated to my wife, Darla, and my three sons, Tony, Matthew, and Gabriel. During the past thirty years they have enjoyed learning these wonderful truths found in the Bible and have used them in their productive lives. I am truly blessed to have such a family whom I love very much and who love me back. I am very proud of all of them and my ultimate wish is that we can all be together in Heaven one day.

Marco A. Martinez
352-239-7697
Marco@30biblicaltruths.com

352-255-4688

ABOUT THE AUTHOR

Marco Martinez was born in El Salvador, Central America. In 1962, when he was three years old, his parents migrated to Los Angeles, California. Raised in inner city Los Angeles, Marco learned many life lessons on the streets. Marco graduated from Belmont High School in 1976 and enlisted in the United States Air Force as an administrative specialist. His first duty station was in Abilene, Texas. He met and married Darla Davis, who was also serving in the Air Force, in November 1977. It was in the city of Abilene that both Marco and Darla were taught the Gospel of Jesus Christ, and each of them surrendered their lives to Christ on October 15, 1979. They have been married for over 36 years and have three children (Tony - age 34, Matthew – age 31, and Gabriel – age 26) and seven wonderful grandchildren.

Since his conversion to Christ, Marco has been involved in many ministries (youth, young adults, evangelism, teaching, lead minister at four different congregations, and chaplain in the Air Force). Marco graduated from the Southern California School of Evangelism in Buena Park, California in 1983. He received his BA in Biblical Studies from Abilene Christian University in Abilene, Texas in 1990. His graduate work took place at Pepperdine University in California, where he received his MA in ministry in 1991. Marco also completed his postgraduate work at Pepperdine University in 1993. Because of his exceptional record in the Air Force and his educational accomplishments, Marco received a presidential appointment from President Bill Clinton in 1997 and was awarded a commission as a First Lieutenant in the Air Force Reserves serving in the role of Chaplain. Marco continued serving in the

Air Force Reserves until December 2003, at which time he retired at the rank of Captain. Marco loves teaching both the lost and the saved. He also enjoys helping both small and large churches through messages of encouragement.

So that your trust may be in the LORD, I teach you today, even you. Have I not written thirty sayings for you, sayings of counsel and knowledge, teaching you to be honest and to speak the truth, so that you bring back truthful reports to those you serve? (Proverbs 22:19-21)

CONTENTS

Dedication		5
About the Author		7
Preface		11
Introduction		13
1	Ask and You Shall Receive	17
2	Use What You Have	29
	Don't Worry About What You Don't Have	
3	Truth Brings Freedom	39
4	You Become Like Your Associations	51
5	What You Plant is What You Harvest	61

PREFACE

This book assumes that the many biblical truths found in God's Word can and will bless the reader if he or she will use them in daily life. The Word of God is not only powerful, but also very practical and useful. All we have to do is learn from God's Word and use it in our daily lives to be blessed.

The Wise and Foolish Builders

"Therefore everyone who hears these words of mine and puts them into practice is like a wise man who built his house on the rock. The rain came down, the streams rose, and the winds blew and beat against that house; yet it did not fall, because it had its foundation on the rock. But everyone who hears these words of mine and does not put them into practice is like a foolish man who built his house on sand. The rain came down, the streams rose, and the winds blew and beat against that house, and it fell with a great crash." (Matthew 7:24-27)

INTRODUCTION

The purpose of this book is to impart to you, the reader, powerful truths that will open a portal to a life filled with positive opportunities and happiness. Most importantly, it is to impart principles that will help you achieve a blessed, meaningful life. These principles are like gems or precious stones that are of great value. I did not come up with these truths on my own. I only serve as one who uses these biblical teachings with great gratitude, and I now share this biblical treasure with you.

I discovered these principles as I was teaching biblical facts and truths to new converts. I shared many concepts with them, but often felt that they needed quick, practical instruction in the faith. These principles are easy to learn and can be applied the very same day they are learned. As I taught these 'big picture truths' to converts, they experienced spiritual growth immediately in their lives. I now want to share thirty of these powerful biblical truths with you so that your life can be blessed. This book represents Volume 1 of my work and contains the first five principles for your learning pleasure.

I realized the power of biblical truth as I read how Jesus replied to the religious Pharisees of His day, who were trying to trap Him by interrogating His beliefs. It is well documented that the religious scholars of Jesus' day argued about which of the over 600 commands of Moses were the greatest. Anytime a person made an assertion about which was the greatest command, it would result in an argument and disagreement. When Jesus was asked which was the most important commandment, He responded that to love God with all of your being (heart, mind, soul, and strength) was the greatest command of all, and to love your neighbor as yourself was just as great (Mark 12:28-31). In other words, Jesus went straight to the overlying principle that no one could dispute. The Apostle Paul recognized the power of this principle and taught the very same truth as the Master. In Romans 13:9, Paul teaches the Roman congregation that the supreme virtue of appropriate conduct toward others can be summed up in one saying: "you shall love your neighbor as yourself."

Another demonstration of the use of practical biblical principles can be found in the Sermon on the Mount, located in Matthew chapters five through seven. In chapter seven, Jesus said the entire law and the teaching of the prophets could be summed up in one principle! He said, "So in everything, do to others what you would have them do to you, for this sums up the Law and the Prophets" (Matthew 7:12). We now call this 'The Golden Rule' simply because we realize the universal power of this great truth. You can apply this teaching immediately in your daily life whether it is at home, at work, or at play and realize it really works!

Each of these examples demonstrate my belief that once a person learns certain biblical principles, he or she can think "from greater to less," applying the principles in specific situations and thereby causing rapid understanding of the Christian faith and its concepts. Sadly, we sometimes teach many good things to others but forget to instruct them on practical truths that make us free. In fact, most so-called 'mature Christians' still haven't learned the wisdom and power of applying these principles in their daily lives. This reality has motivated me to share this knowledge. I now begin the first volume of this six-volume work by sharing with you five of the thirty principles that fulfill my life. My prayer is that you will be blessed by what you read and that your life will be filled with thanksgiving for the wisdom that comes from God's Word.

His Servant and Yours,

Marco A. Martinez
July 2013

Ask and You Shall Receive | 1

"Ask and it will be given to you; seek and you will find; knock and the door will be opened to you. For everyone who asks receives; the one who seeks finds; and to the one who knocks, the door will be opened." (Matthew 7:7-8)

The Biblical Principle

In his ministry, Jesus continually encourages His disciples to ask before receiving, to seek prior to finding, and to knock in order to locate an open door. In the verses cited above, Jesus is clearly speaking of spiritual matters, and promises that the Father is ready and willing to give good things to those who ask Him (Matthew 7:11). Jesus taught us to ask for workers to go into the field (Matthew 9:38), to ask for the Holy Spirit (Luke 11:13), to ask for our daily needs (Matthew 6:11) and to ask for forgiveness (Luke 11:3-4). Jesus also asked the Father on our behalf that we would believe, trust, and be united in Him (John 17:20-23).

The principle of asking is one of the most powerful tools we have to accomplish the will of God. Have you ever read the book of Nehemiah in the Old Testament? Whether you are a corporate officer, city politician, church organizer, group leader, or even a military leader, you can use the knowledge found in the book of Nehemiah to effectively administer any organization or group effort. Amazingly enough, Nehemiah began his work of rebuilding the walls of Jerusalem first by asking God's forgiveness and then by asking for a favor from the King of Persia. The principle of asking God first and then asking our fellow man for help is powerful, and it always leads to greater opportunities.

Let's Talk About it Some More

I remember reading once that life only gives you what you ask of it. Strangely enough, people, especially those creatures known as 'grown-ups,' ask very little of life and therefore receive so little. Ironically, we all know that the way to get more from life begins by asking. Have you ever walked into a child's room and been astonished at the sheer number of toys and gadgets they have acquired over time? Also, notice how many of these purchases transpired after a firm "No!" But how was it that the "no" was converted to a "yes"? You know the answer, don't you? The granting of the requests came by the child's hourly, daily, weekly, monthly, and some cases yearly begging and pleading to their parents. These actions of asking became routine until their requests were finally granted. Little girls and boys, may God bless them all, are filled with so much vision and persistence that they don't ever tire of asking; they don't fear rejection. How is it that adults lose sight of this valuable life principle once they become big people? I'll tell you how it happens; adults teach us that asking too much of others is wrong, shameful, and embarrassing. We are led to believe that asking for something is second-rate and it's better if things come to us naturally. On the traumatic end, we are told that "no" equals rejection, which amounts to failure and low self-esteem... so don't ask any more questions. A child is sadly converted from natural wisdom to what I call 'programmed adult foolishness.' They're instructed to stop asking for things.

I love the story of King Hezekiah in the Bible. His time was up on Earth and he was told by Isaiah the prophet to 'pack his bags' because he only had three days to live. Do you know what

Hezekiah did when he heard this news? He asked God for more time and received it! Consider this story as recorded in the Bible:

In those days Hezekiah became ill and was at the point of death. The prophet Isaiah son of Amoz went to him and said, "This is what the LORD says: Put your house in order, because you are going to die; you will not recover." Hezekiah turned his face to the wall and prayed to the LORD, "Remember, LORD, how I have walked before you faithfully and with wholehearted devotion and have done what is good in your eyes." And Hezekiah wept bitterly. Before Isaiah had left the middle court, the word of the LORD came to him: "Go back and tell Hezekiah, the ruler of my people, 'This is what the LORD, the God of your father David, says: I have heard your prayer and seen your tears; I will heal you. On the third day from now you will go up to the temple of the LORD. I will add fifteen years to your life. And I will deliver you and this city from the hand of the King of Assyria. I will defend this city for my sake and for the sake of my servant David." (II Kings 20:1-6)

The principle of asking has tremendous power when exercised in our daily activities, including the arena of business. In my life, I have supplemented my income by involving myself in a variety of ventures as well as occasionally selling a used car or two. My friend Richard, who worked with the department of corrections in Tehachapi, California, called me one day to tell me that the corrections department would be selling approximately thirty vehicles through a bidding system open to the general public. Richard told me that I could possibly get a great deal on a good quality vehicle, so off I went to the maximum-security prison to 'ask' about this opportunity. Fortunately, the information booth was located at the front gate and the entry guard answered all of my questions. He told me to examine the thirty vehicles in the designated parking area, and if I liked one, to fill out a form stating the amount I wanted to bid on the automobile. My bid would go into a sealed envelope and the highest bidder would receive the car. The parking lot contained a variety of nice cars, trucks, and vans, many of which were fully loaded. At the bidding location I saw dealers, salvage buyers, local residents, and others like myself who were looking for what I call 'parking lot gold.' Rumor was that these vehicles could be purchased at wholesale value, which was about $3,500 per automobile. My goal was to pay as little as possible and at least end up buying one of these vehicles. The dilemma was, which one should I bid on, and what dollar amount should I use to win the bid? I was undecided and running back and forth between vehicles. It was time to ask another question. I asked the woman accepting bids on the lot if I could bid on every car, and she said I could. I then asked what my chances of owning one of these vehicles would be if I placed a bid of $500 per vehicle. She said that there was a remote possibility of winning with my bid, but I should not get my hopes up. She also reminded me that it didn't cost me anything to submit a bid on any of the vehicles, so I should do so anyway. I agreed. Bidding was a form of asking that was written on paper. So I decided to bid on twenty cars and one truck, because I might be blessed if one vehicle was overlooked and no one else placed a bid on it. I would win because my bid, the only bid, would be the highest. After submitting my bids, I went back to my office and waited for a phone call, hoping against all odds that I would be the winner on one vehicle. Guess what happened? I received a call that very same day from the corrections department! My bids were the winning bids on five cars and one truck, for a total cost of $3,000 ($500 per vehicle). I was so thankful for the outcome that I had to pinch myself for a reality check. Thirty days later, I sold all six vehicles for $1,500 each. What started out as an opportunity to buy one vehicle for $500 resulted in a $6,000 profit within thirty days. If my friend would not have told me to ask about the vehicle sale, if I had not asked to bid on several vehicles, if I had not asked... (you can fill in the blanks) nothing would have ever happened. Thank God for the gift of asking!

In the late 1980's I was working as the lead minister at a congregation located in Quartz Hill, California. This band of faithful Christians had saved for many years hoping to someday build a new building, which would be used for classrooms and social gatherings. The amount needed for the construction project was approximately $190,000; the church had raised $10,000 during the past ten years through special collections. There was much discouragement, and hope that a new facility would ever be constructed was fading fast. A local contractor offered to build our new building for $180,000 and he offered the church $60,000 for the corner acre of land that was frontage property (this was extra property owned by the church). Most of the church members were excited about the proposition of adding another $60,000 to the construction fund for the future, but a few of us did not believe this was the answer. I suggested to the group that we should attempt to sell the land ourselves, and maybe we could sell the empty lot for more money to someone else. I vividly remember several members objecting to the foolishness of thinking to ask for more than $60,000 for an empty lot. I argued that it would not hurt to try asking more for the land from the general public; maybe we could attain a greater benefit by this one act. One man named Mel, who was a strong believer of trying anything for the glory of God, spoke up. He stopped the brotherly argument by declaring he would personally post a For Sale sign on the property. After the sign was posted, the telephone was ringing off the hook within one day; the market was hot and many people were interested in the property. One man was especially interested and asked me, "How much are you asking for the property?" I told him that the church was asking $210,000 for the small corner lot. After his initial shock, he informed me that this price was too high, especially since he only needed 15,000 square feet of frontage property. He said he would call me back with a counter-offer. Two days later, he again told me that our asking price was extremely high but that he was willing to pay us $180,000 and not a penny more. I informed him that the church would have to approve of this reduction in price prior to selling him the land. I then asked the church if they would prefer to have $180,000 from the new prospective buyer instead of the $60,000 previously offered by the contractor. After a split second period of prayer, meditation, and deliberation, everyone agreed to accept the $180,000. God saw to it that we built a new building, and not only that, but we ended up with about $20,000 in the bank when all was said and done. Thank God for the little 'For Sale' sign and for people who believed in the power of asking.

Perhaps the people who most recognize the power of asking, apart from children, are people on their deathbeds. It seems that when people realize that life is coming to end, they are reminded of so much they want to get done before they leave this earth. They are sometimes full of regret because of the many things they didn't ask for and receive in their lives. So, guess what they do? They ask those whom they have harmed in the past to forgive them. They ask those whom they are leaving behind to continue to make the most of their lives. They ask loved ones to take care of their children. They ask friends and family to consider changing their ways in light of eternity and to get rid of bad habits such as smoking and drinking. I see all kinds of asking happening in very short order. I believe with all my heart that we should always be 'ask-ful,' not only in death but also in our everyday lives here on earth.

The Objections:

Dignity. Americans of all classes believe that the more you ask, the less dignity and pride you maintain; asking is akin to begging. Many feel that they must stand on their own, depending less and less on others, so they simply don't ask for anything! This belief is nothing but a myth that promotes humanism instead of a well-balanced life. Did Jesus put himself in a shameful position by asking a Samaritan woman for a drink of water? (John 4:7) Why ask for something He could have produced himself? Was this a shameful act? The good Lord knew what he was doing, and by no means did He ever bring shame or disgrace to His name. Pride handicaps us in so many ways. Men are notorious for never wanting to ask for directions when they are lost. They would rather drive aimlessly, wasting time and gasoline, and inflict emotional distress on all their family members in order to avoid asking for help. Some ladies maintain the same conviction as men; they feel that a birthday or anniversary gift means nothing if they must ask for it by reminding their husbands of the special dates. Other ladies never ask for flowers, jewelry, a trip, or even more affection from their mates because they believe asking makes the gift not count as much. What do you think? Does asking invalidate a gift? My response is absolutely not!

Rejection. What about rejection? What if you ask and don't receive? Imagine the horror of rejection and the shame of it all! Well, have you heard the old saying 'nothing ventured, nothing gained'? I have found that we cannot afford to keep silent. Constant fear of rejection is sometimes worse than the actual denial of a request. If we don't ask, we will never receive what we hope for and desire in our hearts. I lived in Buena Park, California while attending the Buena Park School of Biblical Studies in the early 1980s. A boy named Johnny lived next door with his grandmother. One fine sunny afternoon, Johnny was sitting on the front porch of his home with a downcast face for no apparent reason. I asked Johnny why he was so sad and depressed. Johnny had a huge problem he was facing, and no one in the world understood. His school had assigned him the task of selling two boxes of chocolate bars in order to help raise funds for the school. Johnny confessed to me that he feared asking people to buy chocolate bars, but his greater fear was that EVERYONE was going to say NO to his request. He therefore decided to do what most adults would do – nothing! He wouldn't ask anyone to buy his chocolate bars. Sounds pretty silly and foolish, doesn't it? Don't kid yourself; a large number of full-grown productive adults consistently take this same course of action. Johnny and I took a walk to a factory across the street. On Johnny's behalf, I asked the receptionist if any of the plant workers would be interested in buying chocolate bars. Before she could answer, Johnny said, "See, I told you so, no one wants to buy chocolate bars from me, so let's go." The receptionist quickly responded by telling Johnny that the workers happened to love buying the big chocolate almond bars that he was selling. She then announced the boy's arrival to factory workers, and within ten minutes he had sold two boxes of chocolates. Johnny had now completed his assignment in TEN MINUTES. Johnny returned to his school with triumphant news, much to the amazement of his teacher and classmates. The next day, Johnny could be seen selling a fresh box of chocolates in the local neighborhood; his newfound courage allowed him the freedom to knock on neighbors' doors without the fear of rejection. Fear would no longer be his master.

Selfishness and evil. Some believe only selfish people do a great deal of asking. Askers are a lot like beggars, who continually refuse to work and who want others to provide everything for them. This is simply not the case. One must admit that there are many who abuse this principle of success for evil reasons; however, this abuse doesn't negate the positive power of asking. A little passage in James 4:2-3 addresses this matter specifically. James writes, "You do not have, because you do not ask." The passage, of course, is talking about asking for good spiritual things. He continues by declaring "you ask and do not receive, because you ask amiss, that you may spend it on your pleasures." This refers to self-centered asking. We understand that evil people will always be asking for the world on a silver platter, like Herodias' daughter, who asked for the head of John the Baptist (Mark 6:22-23). Now let me ask you something at this juncture: must only the evil people of this world remain the privileged few who harness the power of asking? Is it only drug dealers and pimps who have permission to ask for business? Can good people ask and also receive? Of course we can! If what we request is for the betterment of our lives and the Kingdom of God, then we must ask if we ever expect to receive.

The Application Power

Ask and it *might* be given to you? Wrong! Ask and it *possibly* could be given to you? Wrong again! Ask and it **shall** be given to you? That's what I'm talking about! Both new Christians and those who have dedicated their lives to the cause of the cross want to be more spiritual, prayerful, servant-hearted, evangelistic, forgiven and spirit-filled. Churches want to do more with what little they have. They want to grow, evangelize, believe, share, and support both the needs of the local congregation and missionaries in the field. Employees want more opportunities to advance and to share their ideas with management. Employers want more commitment and dedication from their workers. Wives and husbands want more out of their relationship with one another and with their families. Children want parents who are willing to spend time with them. Grandparents would love to see their children and grandchildren on a regular basis. The world is filled with people needing some type of help to live a more balanced life. We must all use the blessing of asking daily, and we must be persistent if we want the impossible to become possible. One of my favorite stories in the Bible is the one in which Jesus tells about the persistent widow (Luke 18:1-8). The woman keeps asking and asking for justice until she finally gets it. It is noteworthy to realize that Jesus tells this story to encourage His disciples never to grow weary in prayer, the place where we make our requests known to God. Do you truly want to get more out of life? Then why not ask more out of life? Do yourself a favor this week. Ask for something good from someone else, something that you would like someone to do for you. I am not speaking of selfish desires, but of things that promote the Kingdom of God in your life. Ask your enemy to declare peace, ask your loved ones to love you more, ask to be forgiven, ask for a greater opportunity at home, work, or at church. Ask to be used in a greater way. If you're a single young person and you find yourself deeply attracted to someone you admire, why not ask if you can share some time with them? Ask for justice, ask for courage, ask for purity, ask for wisdom, ask for knowledge, ask for peace, ask for joy, and ask most of all for a vision that lets you see beyond your present situation.

The Word of God Section

"LORD, the God of heaven, the great and awesome God, who keeps his covenant of love with those who love him and keep his commandments, let your ear be attentive and your eyes open to hear the prayer your servant is praying before you day and night for your servants, the people of Israel. I confess the sins we Israelites, including myself and my father's family, have committed against you… Lord, let your ear be attentive to the prayer of this your servant and to the prayer of your servants who delight in revering your name. Give your servant success today by granting him favor in the presence of this man. I was cupbearer to the king." (Nehemiah 1:5-6; 11)

"One thing I ask from the LORD, this only do I seek: that I may dwell in the house of the LORD all the days of my life, to gaze on the beauty of the LORD and to seek him in his temple. For in the day of trouble he will keep me safe in his dwelling; he will hide me in the shelter of his sacred tent and set me high upon a rock." (Psalm 27:4-5)

"Jesus went through all the towns and villages, teaching in their synagogues, proclaiming the good news of the kingdom and healing every disease and sickness. When he saw the crowds, he had compassion on them, because they were harassed and helpless, like sheep without a shepherd. Then he said to his disciples, "The harvest is plentiful but the workers are few. Ask the Lord of the harvest, therefore, to send out workers into his harvest field." (Matthew 9:35-38)

"… Now is your time of grief, but I will see you again and you will rejoice, and no one will take away your joy. In that day you will no longer ask me anything. Very truly I tell you, my Father *will give you whatever you ask in my name. Until now you have not asked for anything in my name. Ask and you will receive, and your joy will be complete." (John 16:22-24)*

"What causes fights and quarrels among you? Don't they come from your desires that battle within you? You desire but do not have, so you kill. You covet but you cannot get what you want, so you quarrel and fight. You do not have because you do not ask God. When you ask, you do not receive, because you ask with wrong motives, that you may spend what you get on your pleasures." (James 1:1-3)

Use What You Have | 2
Don't Worry About What You Don't Have

"For if the willingness is there, the gift is acceptable according to what one has, not according to what one does not have." (II Corinthians 8:12)

The Biblical Principle

The Apostle Paul knows how to use words to move a person to action. In II Corinthians 8, Paul encourages Christians to live up to their promise of giving to the needy in Judea. The cross of Christ is at the center of his encouragement as he reminds Christians that it was Jesus who became poor for their sake, and that they now possess a newfound wealth of redemption. Paul continues to reason that this should motivate Christians in Corinth to give abundantly to others. In the midst of this powerful chapter on generosity and love, there is a biblical truth which is often overlooked by readers. Paul declares that if one has a willing mind, God will accept WHAT YOU HAVE and NOT WHAT YOU DON'T HAVE.

This often-overlooked principle of using what we have for the glory of God is a powerful truth that allows the small to become enormous, the insignificant to become substantial, the impossible to become reality, and the simple to evolve into the magnificent. This truth reminds us that if we plant a seed, in time, it can and will become a tree.

Let's Talk About it Some More

I often find myself in conversations with people of all walks of life, occupations, and educational levels. I hear crippling words of negativism in their vocabularies. They cry out, "If I only had more!" and "If only I could be like that person!" The "if I only" philosophy is what I term *phony bologna thinking*. The person who only ruminates on what he does not have produces no fruit. What we don't have will not and cannot help us. Nothing always produces nothing; only God can make something out of nothing. As human beings, we must begin with what we have - not with what we don't have!

The story of teenaged David fighting against Goliath is a wonderful example of someone using what he had. In I Samuel 17, we read the account of the mighty Philistine, Goliath, who challenged the military might of Israel. Israel's experienced veterans thought they needed more than what they had in order to defeat Goliath. They needed a few fighter planes with heat seeking missiles and a couple of armored tanks, but they didn't have this, so the job simply could not be done. Goliath mocked Israel daily and arrogantly boasted of his might over the children of God. But then came the young teenager David with his sling. David felt he could do the job.

He said to King Saul, "Your servant has been keeping his father's sheep. When a lion or a bear came and carried off a sheep from the flock, I went after it, struck it, and rescued the sheep from its mouth. When it turned on me, I seized it by its hair, struck it and killed it. Your servant has killed both the lion and the bear; this uncircumcised Philistine will be like one of them, because he has defied the armies of the living God." Then he took his staff in his hand, chose five smooth stones from the stream, put them in the pouch of his shepherd's bag and, with his sling in his hand, approached the Philistine (I Samuel 17:34-36; 40).

Do you see the principle at work? David didn't have a mighty spear or sword, but he knew God was always with him. He didn't need a tank or a fighter plane; he only needed God to guide one stone into the head of Goliath. He did have a sling, and five smooth stones (one to defeat Goliath and the other four for his four brothers), and a faith in God that believed he could do anything with God on his side. This was more than enough. Using what he had, David was victorious over Goliath and the Philistines. The impossible was now reality.

My family migrated to the United States from Central America when I was just three years old. I learned quickly that others had so much more than we did, but this helped me to realize the beauty of using the resources I had. Forget about what others had; I learned to value what was available to me. When hunger pains hit the old tummy, there was little meat in the refrigerator or snacks to devour like others had. I must confess that what was available to me was a fantastic delicacy that only a certain few are privileged to enjoy: mustard sandwiches. Two pieces of bread and a squirt or two of mustard was both satisfying and very filling once washed down with a little Kool-Aid. Sure, it would have been nice to have a whopper with cheese, French fries, and a Diet Coke (GO LARGE at that), but the mustard sandwich did the job just fine. I had to make do with what was available, and amazingly enough, I also enjoyed it in the process.

One game I loved to play as a child was the survival game. I would go to MacArthur Park in Los Angeles and pretend that I was homeless like the many people I met at the park. My first and foremost task was to survive. The park had a nice little lake stocked with all kinds of fish. I came with no tackle or bait. My assignment was to find some fishing string, a hook, and a small rock to use as a weight. People always threw away items like these when their lines got tangled or caught on a tree branch. Once I found these items, I went to the grassy area and dug for earthworms. The next step was to fish with the string in hand. I would normally catch a Sunfish within minutes. I then cut the Sunfish into many little pieces with my small pocketknife, which then became my fresh bait. I would fish for hours and catch a multitude of fish; it was so much fun! Then when I was fished-out, I could always find someone who was willing to give a nickel a fish. This sales transaction provided me with a steady income of $1 to $2 per fishing adventure. I then used my income to buy a couple of comic books and a great lunch (in the late 1960's a buck went a long way). When I finally came home in the late afternoon, I was always amazed how using the little that was available to me resulted in such a fulfilling day. Life was, and still is, good - even when you think you have so little.

Have you ever heard the story of George Pepperdine, the famous millionaire who founded Western Auto Supply Company and Pepperdine University in Los Angeles, California? Let's go back in time to 1908 when George was only about 23 years old. George knew he had no fortune or fame that would allow him to sit at ease, but instead of worrying about how difficult the Kansas life was in the early 1900s and all the things he did not have, George focused on what he did have. His vast wealth of capital consisted of $5. George took his $5 and purchased 500 one-cent stamps. He then used these stamps on 500 circulars (we call these post cards now), which he mailed out to owners of people who purchased the recently invented automobile. George simply asked these new car owners in his circulars if they needed parts for their vehicles. If so, he said, he could secure it for them at a very reasonable price. This offer was very appealing to recipients because there were no automotive parts stores during this time. Automobile owners soon wrote George time and time again, sending both orders and cash. George took their orders and filled them with inventory stocked at the vendor's location; he didn't even have his own inventory at first. This small experiment became such a success that George Pepperdine opened up his own little store, which stocked a small inventory of goods. Years later, he opened a chain of Western Auto stores all around the United States which made him a multi-millionaire. It all started with a willing mind and five dollars!

The United States government and its employees are sometimes considered the biggest bureaucrats who can't think on their feet and who know very little about anything. Well, I take this rather personally since I have served both on active duty with the Air Force and in the reserves with the Air National Guard for over 20 years. I am proud to say that I have served with some of the brightest, loyal, and hardest working Americans throughout the years. The United States military is the best disciplined, trained, and respected force on the face of the Earth; may God continue to use this force as a deterrent to evil. Periodically, I was required to take an expedient methods class. What kind of class is this, you ask? The class is designed to remind you to constantly use what you have and not to worry about what you don't have. For example, if your fellow airman is bleeding and you have no bandages, cut your undershirt into strips and rescue your friend. If you have no tent to sleep in, dig a hole or find a cave for your temporary accommodations. Want to leave a message on the ground so that a plane can spot you, but you have no marking equipment? Use rocks or branches to spell words. You have no food or water and are all alone in the desert of a foreign land? Eat insects, trap dew with plastic material for water, and eat tree roots. When you find yourself all alone and surrounded by the enemy, call on God; He can always be found, and you will never feel alone. You learn that you can survive almost any situation as long as you know how to use your available resources.

The Objections:

What Difference Can My Small Efforts Make? Many people are convinced that what they can contribute or accomplish in this life is insignificant in light of the whole, and that their efforts are a mere drop in the bucket. Well, I remember that excellent Parable of the Talents found in Matthew 25:14-30. A talent was a certain sum of money, which equals about 91 pounds of a commodity (gold, silver, or bronze). The master left three servants a certain amount of talents (money, bucks, greenbacks... you get the message) according to each one's ability. The first was given five talents, the second three, and the third man one talent. The first two were exceptional businessmen who multiplied their investment, but the third will be forever remembered as the "wicked and lazy servant." What evil crime did this third man commit? His infamous act was the sin of doing NOTHING with what he had. Instead of using his gift in a productive, responsible way, he buried his money in the ground for safekeeping. He could have at least deposited this money at the local bank and drawn a little interest! This third man thought that merely protecting the money in a safe place would bring satisfaction to his master, but instead it produced words of condemnation. This tragic tale is repeated daily in the lives of people all around the world. They do nothing because in their minds, only great commendable deeds are worthwhile and significant. The world would truly be a terrible place without the small things that make it all worthwhile. A hug, a handshake, a smile, a kind word of encouragement, a hospital visit and a cup of water are all small things that can mean a great deal more to a person than all the fame and money this world has to offer. For heaven's sake, do something with your talents and blessings. Nothing used in service to God and humanity is ever a waste of time, no matter how small the act.

What's The Use? I Can't Do Very Much With So Little. When the odds are stacked against you, you can't help but to wonder about the value of your actions in light of life's circumstances. I remember the story in John 6:1ff where Jesus asked his disciples how the crowd of over 5,000 (not including women and children) would be fed. Andrew put it to Him this way: "Here is a boy with five small barley loaves and two small fish, but how far will they go among so many?" (John 6:9) Andrew must have felt that the demand was too great, and the supply so little that what this boy had to offer was not even worth considering. Do you remember how the story ends? Jesus took the bread, blessed it, and multiplied it, and all, yes all, were fed! In the hands of God, today's small efforts become the tomorrow's unbelievable accomplishments. How many people never continue their education because they think one class at a time will get them nowhere? With this reasoning, they never even try. How many businesses were never started because someone's fear of not having enough was greater than their belief in the possibility? How many marriages could have been saved with small acts of love? How many suicide victims would still be alive if, minutes before their death, they found someone to share a few words of hope with them? Remember, every significant thing ever accomplished in the story of humanity begins with small deeds that have no semblance of the mighty feats they eventually become over time.

But It Would Be So Much Easier If I Only Had More! There is no denying this fact. But life has a way of constantly challenging us to grow by placing things before us that are just outside our reach. We cannot advance to this next level of maturity without a meaningful struggle that leads to growth. Sure, it would be easier if a baby didn't have to learn to walk, nourish himself, or speak. It is only when we use what we have to its fullest capacity that we realize growth, independence, and eventually interdependence with one another. Ironically, we will ultimately end up having more through the constant use of what we have. The belief that something easier is of greater value than that which causes us to struggle is a myth.

The Application Power

What resources do you have? What gifts has God given you? What opportunities are before you? I am always amazed at people who come to the United States from foreign countries. They come with almost nothing: no cash, no home, no friends, not even a driver's license. Yet a few years later, these new neighbors own homes and cars, and some even start their own businesses! They really teach us how to use all the blessings we take for granted. This is the whole truth and nothing but the truth: we must learn to be THANKFUL for everything we have here in America. Be thankful for our schools, our medical facilities, our powerful institutions, and most of all our freedom to dream, worship, and make something of ourselves. Christians especially need to be mindful of the cross of Christ and the tremendous spiritual blessings we already possess. In spite of our circumstances, we truly are rich and blessed ALWAYS by what we have in Christ (we are forgiven, comforted, strengthened, and alive spiritually). Why not make a list of the people, opportunities, and things you have in your life and give God thanks for all these blessings? Then use what you have, and be grateful for these unique gifts. USE THEM with all your might, and watch how you end up accomplishing so much more than you thought possible. Don't worry about what you don't have; this is so foolish and unproductive. Instead, learn to think in a different way. Remember that God can feed thousands with the few fish you have in your hands! Use what you have and forget about what you don't have.

The Word of God Section

"Early in the morning, Jerub-Baal (that is, Gideon) and all his men camped at the spring of Harod. The camp of Midian was north of them in the valley near the hill of Moreh. The LORD said to Gideon, "You have too many men. I cannot deliver Midian into their hands, or Israel would boast against me, 'My own strength has saved me.' Now announce to the army, 'Anyone who trembles with fear may turn back and leave Mount Gilead.'" So twenty-two thousand men left, while ten thousand remained. But the LORD said to Gideon, "There are still too many men. Take them down to the water, and I will thin them out for you there. If I say, 'This one shall go with you,' he shall go; but if I say, 'This one shall not go with you,' he shall not go." So Gideon took the men down to the water. There the LORD told him, "Separate those who lap the water with their tongues as a dog laps from those who kneel down to drink." Three hundred of them drank from cupped hands, lapping like dogs. All the rest got down on their knees to drink. The LORD said to Gideon, "With the three hundred men that lapped I will save you and give the Midianites into your hands. Let all the others go home." So Gideon sent the rest of the Israelites home but kept the three hundred, who took over the provisions and trumpets of the others." (Judges 7:1-8)

As she was going to get it, he called, "And bring me, please, a piece of bread." "As surely as the LORD your God lives," she replied, "I don't have any bread—only a handful of flour in a jar and a little olive oil in a jug. I am gathering a few sticks to take home and make a meal for myself and my son, that we may eat it—and die." Elijah said to her, "Don't be afraid. Go home and do as you have said. But first make a small loaf of bread for me from what you have and bring it to me, and then make something for yourself and your son. For this is what the LORD, the God of Israel, says: 'The jar of flour will not be used up and the jug of oil will not run dry until the day the LORD sends rain on the land.'" She went away and did as Elijah had told her. So there was food every day for Elijah and for the woman and her family." (I Kings 17:11-15)

"All the days of the oppressed are wretched, but the cheerful heart has a continual feast. Better a little with the fear of the LORD than great wealth with turmoil. Better a small serving of vegetables with love than a fattened calf with hatred." (Proverbs 15:15-17)

"Jesus sat down opposite the place where the offerings were put and watched the crowd putting their money into the temple treasury. Many rich people threw in large amounts. But a poor widow came and put in two very small copper coins, worth only a few cents. Calling his disciples to him, Jesus said, "Truly I tell you, this poor widow has put more into the treasury than all the others. They all gave out of their wealth; but she, out of her poverty, put in everything - all she had to live on." (Mark 12:41-43)

Truth Brings Freedom | 3

"To the Jews who had believed him, Jesus said, "If you hold to my teaching, you are really my disciples. Then you will know the truth, and the truth will set you free." (John 8:31-32)

The Biblical Principle

Jesus, the greatest teacher of all time, taught His disciples tremendous pearls of knowledge and wisdom. In the Gospel of John, John records the words Jesus shared with them, namely that truth brings freedom. There is no doubt that the truth John wants his readers to discover is that Jesus Christ is the Son of God, and that He is the source of eternal life. Amazingly, John uses the word 'truth' in nearly every chapter in the Gospel of John. John wrote,

"Jesus performed many other signs in the presence of his disciples, which are not recorded in this book. But these are written that you may believe that Jesus is the Messiah, the Son of God, and that by believing you may have life in his name." (John 20:30-31)

Christians believe that learning the teachings of Christ results in eternal salvation and deliverance from the deceit and lies of this world. But in order to understand truth, one MUST ABIDE IN THE WORD. Learning and practicing are absolutely essential! The concept that the truth makes us free is so powerful that it proves true not only in spiritual matters, but also in all areas of knowledge (science, medicine, geography, technology, and the list goes on). We need to value truth and knowledge more than physical, earthly riches. Freedom does come from learning truth!

Let's Talk About it Some More

I remember old Bob Irby (one of my instructors at the Southern California School of Evangelism) asking in class, "How free do the teachings of Jesus make you?" My fellow classmates and I pondered the question. We knew the answer was simple yet illusive, because Bob Irby was always in the habit of asking loaded questions. True to form, Bob told us the question was a 'trick question' just like we thought. He told us the answer to his question (how free do the teachings of Jesus make you?) all depended on the answer to a second question. The second question was, "HOW FREE DO YOU WANT TO BE?" He then concluded that the teachings of Jesus could make us as free as we wanted in all areas of our lives, but we had to desire and seek this freedom. In other words, initially the truth makes us free from being lost in sin through Christ. However, Christians have the opportunity to gain additional freedom in so many more areas of their spiritual walk if they desire such freedom in Christ. For example, do you want to overcome anger (the bad kind of anger)? You have to learn how to overcome sinful anger and how to practice self-control. Do you want to leave less room for greed and more space for generosity? Then you have to learn about sharing and actually practice giving to others. The bottom line rests in the simple principle that learning and practicing leads to wonderful freedom! In order to fully appreciate this great principle, let us consider some examples from the secular realm. Please keep in mind that my use of these examples to demonstrate general truths does not imply that I believe they are greater than spiritual examples.

The fourth grade was a wonderful time of discovery for

me. It all started when I was transferred from my original fourth grade classroom to a special gifted program. I clearly remember walking into the classroom filled with a variety of 'eggheads' and abnormal people who would rather eat books than food. At first I was not impressed. I sat with the class that met in the library and found myself surrounded by thousands of books. I remember the teacher asking me what I knew about the Renaissance. I didn't know if this strange word was a disease, a food, or a street name in Los Angeles. I felt even more ignorant and uncomfortable when I discovered that most of the other kids knew what she was talking about, and they even had enough knowledge to carry on a conversation with her on the subject. It was then that the teacher spoke words of comfort loudly and clearly. She told me not to worry, because I could learn about anything I wanted and I could become whatever I learned. She told me to look around the library classroom and observe the wealth of knowledge that was at my fingertips, if only I was willing to research and grow. She pointed the way to freedom, and I was young enough to believe her. I had books at home that belonged to my mother, including the family encyclopedia set. I first began by attempting to read the big dust-covered book called 'The Holy Bible,' but my mother told me that I was too young to attempt to study something as sacred as the Bible. So I went on to the next set of books, the encyclopedias. Was the teacher right when she said I could learn anything I wanted to know simply by reading? Well, I spent months reading about everything from A to Z. I read about Einstein, nuclear energy, reproduction, the Civil War, minerals, and animals, and my favorite part of the entire encyclopedia was the section on anatomy which came with clear plastic sheets depicting the various systems of the body and its organs. I loved it all! Whenever I asked others questions about certain things like drug abuse, the human reproductive cycle, steam engines, and the like, people responded by telling me I was too young to want to know about these matters. I would then hit the books and find plenty of answers that helped me understand more and more about life. When my little friends had some serious questions about life, I always helped them out by reading on the matter and then presenting the information to them - this was always worth a cookie or two. Can you imagine how many more cookies I could have earned if I had the Internet back then? My teacher was right, and to this day I owe her and everyone else who has shared their knowledge with me a great debt of gratitude.

I get a kick out of watching women in action. My wife Darla has provided me with many years of fascinating entertainment. The principle that truth sets us free can be observed in her ravenous desire to acquire great and unique recipes. Darla, like most ladies, will usually try a food dish with which she is unfamiliar. If this new discovery takes place at a potluck, she immediately wants to know who made the dish. She then finds the person and asks what ingredients it contains and how it is prepared. She ultimately asks, "Can I have the recipe?" When we eat at a restaurant, Darla has me interrogating the waitress, the cook, and even the dish washer in an attempt to discover the recipe. If all else fails, Darla uses the Internet to research recipes online, or she buys recipe books - she has a ton of them. The point I'm making here is that knowledge of recipes allows Darla the freedom to recreate any dish she has ever tasted. Can you see what great freedom learning brings, even with regard to cooking?

Truth Brings Freedom

God has blessed me with the privilege of knowing many amazing people who serve society in various fields like religion, business, medicine, and education. In the area of business, I have been honored to work directly for around a dozen multi-millionaires at different times throughout my life. All of these men and women have shared fundamental knowledge and business truths with me that have empowered me to secure greater employment opportunities. None of these unique individuals have accomplished the task of writing a book, but the reality of the matter is that each of these people are LIVING BOOKS. They contain, within their minds, volumes of books filled with tremendous experience and wisdom. I consider each of these individuals as fountains of business truth; they provided me with mental nourishment. If you want to succeed in business, why not ask a successful businessman or businesswoman how they triumphed over adversity to become successful? I personally can't understand why people constantly want to learn things the hard way by doing it themselves when others have already accomplished the same things successfully in the past. If you've never had an opportunity to meet a successful businessperson, why not buy their books and read about their lives, their principles, and their practices? This will accomplish the same objective, helping you to learn useful truths which give you the power to grow and prosper.

When I was eighteen years old, I purchased my first brand new car, a little Toyota Corolla. After driving about six months, I took my car in for a tune-up. I asked the mechanic how much he would charge me to do the work. He told me it would cost $49.99 plus tax (this was back in the day). I told him to go ahead with the work, as long as he would allow me to watch him work and teach me how it was done. It took him about 20 minutes to change the four spark plugs and one distributor cap, and do the timing on the engine. Needless to say, I was shocked that I was now nearly $50 poorer just for 20 minutes of work. A year later, when my car was about due for its next tune-up, I drove to the auto parts store and purchased a repair manual, a timing gun, a good supply of spark plugs, a can of carburetor spray cleaner, a distributor cap, a rotor and a small tool kit. It did take me about an hour to do the work, but I was able to do my own tune-up at the cost of about $10 in parts, and labor was free (for the record, the book and timing gun are not included in my ten dollar figure). Because of this great savings discovery, I rarely had to go to a mechanic for a tune-up. Can you imagine the thousands of dollars that mechanic allowed me to save by agreeing to teach me how to do my own tune-up? Knowledge is not just mentally profitable, but often it is economically beneficial as well. I have been able to enjoy the freedom to save money because of the truths the mechanic shared with me.

Scripture contains so many powerful examples that clearly outshine those above. One of my favorites passages is Ephesians 4:17-32, where the Apostle Paul teaches what I call the 'Overcoming the Old Man Via the New Man Substitution Principle.' Paul reminds Christians that they have been TAUGHT (verses 20-21) to get rid of the old person, who was being corrupted by deceitful lust, and put on the new person, who is to be dressed in righteousness and holiness. But how does one complete the assignment to change? Paul addresses this by laying down a spiritual formula for success, which is the substitution principle. Just as the scientific community has discovered that for every action there is an equal and opposite reaction, so Paul teaches that if we have a problem with lying, then we must speak the truth (verse 25). If we have long-term anger and/or sinful behavior attached to our anger, we must learn to defuse it before the day ends and express our anger in constructive ways (verse 26-27). If we once stole from others, we must now work with our hands and give to those who are in need (verse 28). If we used corrupt words to destroy others, we must now use words that build up and encourage (verse 29). In other words, if you're eating too much cake and gaining weight, then eat carrots instead. It is not enough to recognize a destructive habit; we must recognize the old person and counteract it with the opposite person. This gem of truth has the power to help us become what God expects us to be. This truth gives us the ability to become a new person, which glorifies Christ. The teachings of Christ offer so many of these types of powerful truths. Let's use them for the good!

The Objections:

I Am Too Old to Learn Now. It seems that many people believe learning is only for the young. Once we complete high school or college, the learning party is over. It is incredible to see how many adults really believe that 'old dogs can't learn new tricks.' I have met people in their 30's and 40's who regret not pursuing further education; they conclude that they will be stuck earning a meager living and working at entry-level jobs for the rest of their lives. This is crazy thinking! God has made it possible for us to keep learning until the day we die (for the most part). People like 69-year-old Noah Webster, who published Webster's Dictionary, and Grandma Moses, whose painting became popular at the age of 80, are just two examples of so many people who not only continued learning at an old age, but also promoted the desire to continue learning. It is also noteworthy that God used 80-year-old Moses to lead the Israelites to the promised land. Moses went through a great learning period for the next 40 years working with his people while learning the ways of the great 'I Am.' We are also blessed to be living in the 'Information Age,' which allows us to use the Internet to learn anything we want 24 hours a day. What a great tool for those who desire knowledge!

Truth is Relative – We are told by the alleged great thinkers and educators of our time that we are in the 'Post-Modern Age.' Postmodernity proclaims that everything is relative; there is no fundamental truth about anything. What you believe is okay and what I believe is okay, because we have no universal laws of conduct, ethics, religion, or even science that can be labeled as 'absolute truth.' Everything is a matter of your viewpoint and thereby subjective in nature. You have got to be kidding, right? If this is the case, why do we bother to have laws and courts? Why do we have colleges and universities? How are we to make advancements in the fields of medicine, science, history, space exploration, and technology if past information is all relative? Let me tell you this one thing. Biblical truths are real and effective; they are not relative. It will never be right to oppress and mistreat others. It will always be right to take care of widows and orphans. God's biblical truths never grow old.

Truth is Hard to Find. Some people think that real truth is hard to discover. They have a hard time trusting others and an even tougher time allowing others to teach them. They would rather spend countless hours surfing the Internet, reading all kinds of useless articles about famous celebrities or chatting with people they have never met about stuff that is useless. These 'seekers of miscellaneous trivia' would have been better off being born as birds, since they enjoy 'tweeting' all day long – what a waste of the precious gift of time God has given us. I have found that we can gain great knowledge by spending time with older people, especially older Christians. They have life experiences that are practical, resourceful, and most importantly, spiritual. I have found great mentors at church who generously gave me their years of wisdom and knowledge. With this in mind, it is hard to believe that our modern society finds no value in being part of the church. Also, as previously mentioned, the Internet is a powerful resource for you to learn all kinds of helpful information. Books are fantastic resources, especially to increase your knowledge of the Christian faith, overcome addictions and emotional hang-ups, study history, and gain general knowledge. We live in a great age in which we can acquire knowledge to help us make our world a better place, if we would just seek truth in all realms of life.

The Application Power

The truth can make you free. There are so many fields of study which are of great benefit to mankind, but for me, the greatest truths involve the Kingdom of God. We need to be students of the Bible, and we need to learn how to be free in all aspects of our lives. This means we have to put an effort into learning and studying; this will cost us our precious time, but it will be worth every minute. Once we learn and practice these godly truths, we need to share this knowledge with our family members and then with the world.

Personally, seeking the truth about the topics listed below has given me the most joy in my life. I challenge you to consider these matters now.

- I can't save myself; it is only through the blood of Christ that I am saved.
- I can change my bad habits and become a new person in Christ because of His Holy Spirit that dwells in me, and through the teachings found in Scripture.
- I can stop thinking only about my earthly existence and I can meditate on the eternal world, which exists now and in the life to come, because it is of greater importance.
- I can forgive others because I have been forgiven.
- I can learn and grow in my Christian faith through study and prayer.
- I can have a support group for all my problems if I am connected with the church, which is my spiritual family.
- I can learn how to not be worried about the things of this world, which are perishing and temporary.
- I can teach others the good things taught to me.
- I need the grace of God daily because no matter how mature I become, I still fall short of the glory of God.
- I have learned to not waste time on trivial matters.
- I have learned that other people know so much more than me in so many areas, and I need to trust them to help me overcome the problems in my life.
- I have learned that we are all 'messed up' in one fashion or another, and we need to help each other.

The Word of God Section

"LORD, who may dwell in your sacred tent? Who may live on your holy mountain? The one whose walk is blameless, who does what is righteous, who speaks the truth from their heart; whose tongue utters no slander, who does no wrong to a neighbor, and casts no slur on others." (Psalm 15:1-3)

"Listen to your father, who gave you life, and do not despise

your mother when she is old. Buy the truth and do not sell it—wisdom, instruction and insight as well. The father of a righteous child has great joy; a man who fathers a wise son rejoices in him." (Proverbs 23:22-24)

"Thomas said to him, "Lord, we don't know where you are going, so how can we know the way?" Jesus answered, "I am the way and the truth and the life. No one comes to the Father except through me. If you really know me, you will know my Father as well. From now on, you do know him and have seen him." (John 14:5-7)

"For in the gospel the righteousness of God is revealed—a righteousness that is by faith from first to last, just as it is written: "The righteous will live by faith." The wrath of God is being revealed from heaven against all the godlessness and wickedness of people, who suppress the truth by their wickedness, since what may be known about God is plain to them, because God has made it plain to them." (Romans 1:17-19)

"Now we pray to God that you will not do anything wrong—not so that people will see that we have stood the test but so that you will do what is right even though we may seem to have failed. For we cannot do anything against the truth, but only for the truth. We are glad whenever we are weak but you are strong; and our prayer is that you may be fully restored." (II Corinthians 13:7-9)

"Therefore put on the full armor of God, so that when the day of evil comes, you may be able to stand your ground, and after you have done everything, to stand. Stand firm then, with the belt of truth buckled around your waist, with the breastplate of righteousness in place, and with your feet fitted with the readiness that comes from the gospel of peace." (Ephesians 6:13-5)

"Keep reminding God's people of these things. Warn them

before God against quarreling about words; it is of no value, and only ruins those who listen. Do your best to present yourself to God as one approved, a worker who does not need to be ashamed and who correctly handles the word of truth. Avoid godless chatter, because those who indulge in it will become more and more ungodly." (II Timothy 2:14-16)

You Become Like Your Associations | 4

"Do not be misled: 'Bad company corrupts good character.'"
(I Corinthians 15:33)

The Biblical Principle

As Paul encourages Christians in Corinth, he reminds them of a popular saying that was widely used and understood in the secular world: 'Bad company can corrupt you!' It is apparent that the teaching on the resurrection was being altered, or maybe completely abandoned, by some of the Christians in Corinth. Paul identifies the root of the problem, the fact that bad company had influenced some of these Corinthians.

Isn't it true that the company a person keeps will, to a large extent, determine what kind of person he or she is or will be? It is clear from reading the book of I Corinthians that these Christians were filled with worldly pollution (sexual immorality, lawsuits against one another, arrogance, and disbelief in the basic Gospel). Paul challenges the Corinthians to conduct a personal inventory of their associations and to discard those friendships that are causing pollution.

Let's Talk About it Some More

I have always been fascinated with different types of people. I made many friendships with both good and bad people growing up. My good friends in high school encouraged me to study, behave, and take part in athletics. The bad friends I had encouraged me to do wrong. What else is there to say? Some of these bad guys and girls were gangsters who loved to do evil. They drank alcohol, smoked marijuana, inhaled PCP, and sniffed paint (inhaling clear spray paint on a white sock produces a temporary high and a permanent killing of brain cells, in case you were wondering). They enjoyed fighting, stealing, defying authority, and even killing other rival gang members, and sadly, I was becoming just like them. My dress, language, and worldview was becoming exactly like theirs. I began to smoke marijuana, steal, and destroy things that belonged to others, and I was basically becoming downright evil. I am so grateful I never had to take part in territorial battles, which usually found a person stabbed or shot (this is one of those privileges reserved for members only; I never joined a gang because I was friends with people in several gangs). I also didn't use hard drugs, but I sure was becoming a lot like my associations. The bottom line is that we are like a mirror image of our associations. Let me stop right here to define associations. Many people define associations as someone you spend time with during the course of your day-to-day activities. Well, I believe that the TV programs you watch, the people you call on the phone or chat with on the Internet, the people with whom you share your time, and the books/magazines you read are your ASSOCIATIONS. What do all of these activities (TV, Internet, books, etc.) have in common? They are types of communication that speak to our minds and consume our thought faculties. We are what we think about; we become what we dwell on.

Why do magazine companies sell millions of dollars' worth of magazines filled with photos and printed words? Because they contain information about people we love and admire. These people are the ones we generally want to be like; they are our models, who we want to imitate in one way or another. Why do our kids buy Nike? Is it because they are the best sport shoes in the world? I think not. It is because the best athletes wear them. What a racket the advertising world works on us! Association is a powerful determiner of one's character. Evil people will pollute you in one form or another. Have you ever washed a black shirt or a dark sweater together with whites? Have you ever spilled Clorox on your colored clothing? Combinations such as these remind us that associations do have a direct impact, just as our 'people associations' have a direct impact on our minds.

Have you ever laid in bed and thought about young Alexander the Great and how he conquered the world in his early thirties? I have, and I continue to be amazed at Alexander's determination, leadership, vision, and power, not to mention the tremendous conquest he undertook for the Grecian Empire. Do you know who schooled him in the ways of religion, politics, mathematics, philosophy, and military conquest? It was the great Greek philosopher Aristotle. Aristotle's exceptional mind was within Alexander in one way or another. Alexander's gifts were partly bestowed upon him by God at birth, and then acquired through his schoolmaster Aristotle. Alexander was also influenced by the sexual vices of his world and therefore had sexual relationships with other men, which is both unfortunate and ungodly. Would Alexander have been as great of a military and political leader without the training and teaching of Aristotle? We will never know, but I believe that history would have recorded a different story if Alexander had been raised by a bunch of drunkards. Each one of us is influenced in either a positive or negative way by our past and present associations. This cannot be denied. What you shall become in the future is determined by the associations you have now or the ones you will form in the future. This is a reality.

Did you know that for every action there is an equal and opposite reaction? I think Mr. Fig Newton came up with this a long time ago (it may have been Sir Isaac Newton). All joking aside, Newton was really on the ball, and I must admit I have been impressed with his findings almost on a daily basis (no joke). Just observing my daily actions of eating, breathing, and walking, I am reminded of Isaac Newton. By the way, have you heard about Marco's law of semi-knowledge, which declares that every positive or negative fact statement contains a reversal declaration of that same statement? Now, I know I made this explanation up in my head, but it's true. If you have a little girl and you tell her that eating too much junk is bad, you are also implying that non-junk food will be good for her. When you tell others that you will never use 87 octane rated gasoline in your car because of the poor performance, you are implying that a higher octane is what you will always use because it has a greater performance ratio. Now enough of this mumbo-jumbo; let us get to the point. Using this bipolar logic, Paul not only declares in I Cor. 15:33 that bad company corrupts good character, but he also implies that good company promotes good habits. Did you understand the way I figured this out? There is another side to the statement, "bad company ruins good morals." Inscribed on the other side of the coin is, "good company promotes good habits."

Good company does inspire and move us to a greater level. When I lived in Indiana, my family and I attended a performance by the South Bend Symphony Orchestra. I don't know about you, but whenever a group of musicians gather together to play musical instruments, I get a feeling of excitement and encouragement that motivates me to excellency. Have you ever listened to a sermon spoken with such conviction and power that you wanted to jump up and move to action that very instant? Or, has someone shared a word or two of encouragement that moved you so much that your entire worldview changed? All of us have been touched by good company that builds us up. Sometimes I don't think the church really understands the fact that we gather together to be encouraged. When visiting congregations or listening to Christian radio stations, I can't help but to wonder what is going on! It seems some are dedicated to the idea that we are all created equally to be doomed to boring and discouraging lessons. I have visited many congregations who had this effect on me. When I come to a place of worship that is discouraging in its proclamation, I can't help to feel a sense of great sadness.

I see families come to worship at these places with great anticipation of hearing encouraging songs and a sermon of exhortation. They get up early, speedily dress and round up the kids; they have a little pre-church argument and toast with jelly before arriving to the building... and for what? A spiritless and discouraging sermon and a dull songfest. What a waste! We come together to be uplifted and to be surrounded by great company; this is what going to worship means. Now, if you're a grumpy and negative person, you are already thinking that I am nothing but an unrealistic man, a level nine optimist living in a dream world. Well, the last time I checked the Scriptures they read like this:

"Let us not give up meeting together as some are in the habit of doing, but let us encourage one another - and all the more as you see the Day approaching." (Hebrews 10:25)

Now this hortatory message tells me that CHRISTIANS should be encouragers, and I believe this. We should be the best company others have ever had. People should be provoked by our good deeds and thereby give God the glory. The church should be the best company in the world.

Let's go back to the principle that your associations have direct influence on you. I love going to garage sales and estate sales. The people who have these types of sales don't realize it, but they want to sell you the things with which they wish to disassociate themselves. People want to sell you all kinds of merchandise for next to nothing: CD players, tools, clothing, books, jewelry, and the like. They sell these things for next to nothing because to them, they are worth exactly that – next to nothing. When I go to estate sales, I don't want to know who lived in the house where the auction is taking place - at least not in the beginning. I go through the entire house examining wardrobes, books and magazine racks, movies and videos they watched, toys they played with (yes, every adult still has toys, but they are called valuables/collectibles), the pictures they've posted on their walls, and the many other things they have displayed in their home. After conducting this investigation, I come to some conclusions about this person's identity and character. I generally get pretty close, and I am always reminded to think about what is in my house and what the Lord Jesus will think when he does His inventory of my residence. Well, we need Him to find good associations in our lives. We must choose to associate ourselves with good and noble people, not for their sake, but for ours.

The Objections

It's Hard to Find Good Associations. Some people believe that everyone has low moral standards these days, and therefore it is impossible to find good people with whom to associate. This simply is not the case. It all depends on where you go to find friends. If you regularly spend time in a bar, you can expect drunkenness, sexual immorality, fits of rage, jealously, anger, and disputes. Yes, there will also be friendships, relaxation, community, and a sense of belonging at the bar scene, but these will be combined with the things already mentioned that can pollute you. Why place yourself in an environment with so many bad associations and temptations? People who find it hard to find good associations often refuse to change their friendships; they keep hanging out with people who love the world and its pleasure. You must give up bad habits and friends and find new ones. Addicts often join organizations such as AA or Celebrate Recovery in order to belong to a new set of friends who are devoted to overcoming their past lives and temptations. They encourage each other to meet in a friendly environment for fellowship and encouragement, thereby avoiding places that make them weak. A good place to find connections is the church; it is the place where you find godly people challenging you to be different. These spiritual people want you to go to heaven and will encourage you not to associate with anyone who threatens your salvation in Christ.

Good Associations Rarely Know How to Have Fun.

Some people believe that 'well behaving people' just can't have fun. They associate a person who is godly with someone who is 'boring' and who has no fun at all. Why are they boring? They are boring because they don't lose control, they watch what they say, they respect themselves, they believe in being a positive influence on society, and they stay faithful to their wives or husbands. They believe spending time with their children is better than getting drunk; they make good use of their time; they save their money; they refuse to be intoxicated with drugs or alcohol because of the consequences associated with these additions; they refuse to be contaminated with sexually transmitted diseases such as AIDS and herpes. This is why they basically don't know how to enjoy the so-called 'good life' and have a 'good time.' Therefore, these good associations are considered 'boring.' Come on, let's be real! A godly person or group will be different than the world, but they are not boring. They like different entertainment that is good, clean fun. What is wrong with going to dinner, the movies, the park, the beach, or a theme park? What's wrong with bowling, hiking, exercising, attending a Bible study, or even grabbing a cup of coffee? The problem is not that good people are boring. The problem rests with those who call evil deeds 'fun' and good deeds 'boring.'

The Application Power

Would you like to be a great auto mechanic? Buy good automotive repair books and spend time with a good mechanic. Would you like to be a successful salesperson? Attend seminars given by successful salespeople and listen to CDs promoted by businesspeople. Better yet, spend some time with a great salesperson. Want to learn about the cosmos and about the universal formulas of science? Spend time at the university with a good professor, or read the publications of great scientists or physics professors. Do you want to be a miserable, selfish, evil person with a bad attitude? Then surround yourself with these kinds of individuals; they will be glad to teach you the tricks of their trade! How sad, and what a waste! I think you get the message. Spend time, or shall I say, associate yourself with those whom you want to imitate, and guess what? You will eventually become like them.

Spiritually speaking, always attend worship services, because you are associating yourself with eternal things such as songs of praise, prayer, revelation from God's word, remembrance of Jesus' sacrifice through the Lord's Supper, and brotherly love found in fellow Christians. Also, get involved in regular Bible study, as this will increase your spiritual knowledge and remind you to abstain from the lust of the flesh and worldly influences. Attending other events such as workdays at the building, breakfast meetings, and social events sponsored by the church are also excellent opportunities to grow in godliness and avoid being polluted by the world.

I remember Jesus saying that the disciple becomes like his teacher. I have now come to realize that you can only be as great as those from whom you learn. May God help us to continually choose good models to imitate, and may He grant us wisdom and strength to avoid those associations that will ruin us.

The Word of God Section

"A longing fulfilled is sweet to the soul, but fools detest turning from evil. Walk with the wise and become wise, for a companion of fools suffers harm. Trouble pursues the sinner, but the righteous are rewarded with good things." (Proverbs 12:19-21)

"Three days later Jeroboam and all the people returned to Rehoboam, as the king had said, "Come back to me in three days." The king answered the people harshly. Rejecting the advice given him by the elders, he followed the advice of the young men and said, "My father made your yoke heavy; I will make it even heavier. My father scourged you with whips; I will scourge you with scorpions." (I Kings 12:12-14)

"When they saw the courage of Peter and John and realized that they were unschooled, ordinary men, they were astonished and they took note that these men had been with Jesus." (Acts 4:13)

"When Cephas came to Antioch, I opposed him to his face, because he stood condemned. For before certain men came from James, he used to eat with the Gentiles. But when they arrived, he began to draw back and separate himself from the Gentiles because he was afraid of those who belonged to the circumcision group. The other Jews joined him in his hypocrisy, so that by their hypocrisy even Barnabas was led astray." (Galatians 2:11-13)

"This is a trustworthy saying. And I want you to stress these things, so that those who have trusted in God may be careful to devote themselves to doing what is good. These things are excellent and profitable for everyone. But avoid foolish controversies and genealogies and arguments and quarrels about the law, because these are unprofitable and useless. Warn a divisive person once, and then warn them a second time. After that, have nothing to do with them." (Titus 3:8-10)

"Therefore, since Christ suffered in his body, arm yourselves also with the same attitude, because whoever suffers in the body is done with sin. As a result, they do not live the rest of their earthly lives for evil human desires, but rather for the will of God. For you have spent enough time in the past doing what pagans choose to do—living in debauchery, lust, drunkenness, orgies, carousing and detestable idolatry. They are surprised that you do not join them in their reckless, wild living, and they heap abuse on you. But they will have to give account to him who is ready to judge the living and the dead. For this is the reason the gospel was preached even to those who are now dead, so that they might be judged according to human standards in regard to the body, but live according to God in regard to the spirit." (I Peter 4:1-6)

What You Plant is What You Harvest | 5

"Do not be deceived: God cannot be mocked. A man reaps what he sows. Whoever sows to please their flesh, from the flesh will reap destruction; whoever sows to please the Spirit, from the Spirit will reap eternal life." (Galatians 6:7-8)

The Biblical Principle

It seems everyone has heard this principle in one form or another. Some people call it 'The Law of the Farm.' In Galatians 6:7, the apostle Paul writes that a man reaps what he sows. Isn't that the truth? This is a great truth - a man or woman does reap whatever he or she sows.

Let's Talk About it Some More

You reap what you sow. That sounds simple. When I was a kid I loved to plant vegetables, and I did this because I had watched my neighbor plant and grow a great assortment of plants, and I saw the fruit that he would harvest. So at the ripe-old age of eight, I started my planting adventure. I started with a tomato plant. I experienced great joy seeing tomato plants pop out of the ground and begin to grow very quickly. Then I started to get impatient and frustrated, because even though the plant had grown very tall and wide, I still had no fruit. Finally, when the flower appeared and the fruit developed, I was the happiest kid on earth; I was amazed how a tiny little tomato seed had produced so many tomatoes. In the midst of all this joy, I then began to wonder why I only had tomatoes? I thought maybe one of these vines would produce a watermelon or a lemon – I love these two things also. Why, I wondered, did the tomato plant only produce tomatoes? How did the plant know what fruit to produce? A tough question like this is common for an eight-year-old to ponder. I just couldn't figure it out. My 70-year-old neighbor, who was also the landlord of the house we rented, listened to my concern and laughed at me. He said, "Son, you will never get a watermelon or a lemon unless you plant that kind of seed." And I said, "Well, why? I put seeds in the ground. How does the ground know what to give? Why can't it just work with me and give me a big fat watermelon?" He just laughed again and said, "You have to plant the right seed. If you plant the right seed for that plant, that's what you get. There is no other way around this." Now this might seem elementary or funny or common sense to you. Let me tell you something else that is also funny: life also gives you what you have planted in it. In other words, if you want to have happiness in your life, guess what you are going to have to plant? If you want others to care for you, you have to care for them. If you want to be successful, it won't come accidentally. You have to plant hard work and sacrifice so that you can reap the benefits from it. If you want to rid ulcers from your life, you are going to have to learn how to overcome your uncontrolled anger, and then plant the seeds of control and forgiveness. You see, we are like soil; whatever we plant in our souls is what we will produce. Do you know that most people still don't understand this truth? For example, they think they can take massive quantities of drugs or drink large quantities of alcohol and never be affected by this crop they have planted in their bodies. There are so many people in this world who use their computers to indulge in pornography on the Internet, thinking that "just looking" has no effect on their daily lives. They soon find out how wrong they are as their relationship with their spouse goes sideways quickly. Not only do you damage your relationship with your spouse, but this addiction also promotes child pornography, sex trafficking, and so many other abuses toward women and children. Sadly, planting sexual images inside your mind does produce a terrible crop of destruction.

Back to the point: we will reap what we sow. It shouldn't be a shock to us that we only get tomatoes if we plant only tomato plants. Don't look for watermelons, because it takes a different seed to be planted for this fruit! I am so amazed at how many times people think the way they are going to get ahead or make it in life is to buy that one dollar lottery ticket and hit the big jackpot. I know so many people (including some of my relatives) who would have thousands of dollars in the bank just by not buying those tickets. Now here is the real kicker: if instead of planting hope in a lottery ticket, this same person put their time, money, labor, and effort into a business venture, they would enjoy a better return on their money. There are other people who plant hatred, bitterness, envy, and jealousy day after day and then wonder why they are not able to reap any kindness, love, or forgiveness from the same people they abused. Since we are like soil, we have to plant good things so that the blessings of goodness can be harvested. This truth is so simple yet so powerful.

The Objections:

I Have Done So Much Wrong in the Past. What's the Use? Yes, it's great to believe that planting good seeds will produce good fruit; however, many believe that it is of no consequence to change now, because their past lives have been nothing but evil and sin. They have destroyed their careers, families, friendships, and relationships through their evil habits, and ruined so much that nothing can change their situation. So, they ask, what is the use of changing now? It is true that we cannot change the past, and we cannot go back in time to undo the past. It is also true that we must reap the consequences of our past actions. However, we must keep in mind that if we plant good things now, we will have a better and brighter future. If we have been unkind to many in the past who now hate us, it is also true that if we start practicing kindness to those around us today, we will have people who love us tomorrow. What you sow is what you reap. Just because a farmer planted one type of unprofitable crop for the last 40 years doesn't mean he can't change by planting a new, profitable crop for the next 40 years.

I Don't Know How to Grow a New Garden. Becoming a new person is rather challenging and difficult. When a person wants to become someone completely different, they don't think it can be done because they don't know how. This is understandable thinking, but there is a way. We all need others to help us grow our new garden. Though we may feel alone, we need to ask other strong, mature Christians how to go about beginning anew. Through the Spirit and others, we will be taught how to overcome the old person and become the new man or woman God intends us to be. We cannot possibly do this ourselves. We must find helpers who will teach us biblical truth as we grow our new garden.

The Application Power

So the question is, what do you want to reap in your life? Do you want to produce goodness and blessings? Then plant these seeds in your daily life as you live on this earth. I have counseled many people who say, "I don't understand why I am in this situation. Can you tell me why?" Knowing the principle of sowing and reaping, I already know that they are likely reaping what they have sown. So I go back and ask them to tell me what things they have planted in their lives. They tell me of mistakes they have made, marriages they have ruined, addictions that became their master, attitudes that hurt others, time wasted, opportunities neglected, and a host of so many regrets for things they wish they had done. When an hour or so goes by, the person comes to realize that much of what they have planted in the past was not good. Once they are able to see this reality, they ask, "What shall I do?" I tell them that they need to leave the past in God's hands; He can and will deal with it. What they need to do is to start today and plant a better garden for the future. They need to decide what they want to grow in this new garden. It will take both a resolved mind and great patience, but they will yield a bountiful harvest of these good things as long as they don't get discouraged.

I remember when I first started counseling in ministry. I had a young lady come to me for counseling. She said, "I have a problem." So I asked her, "What's the matter?" She said, "I'm pregnant." I then asked her, "How did this happen?" She answered, "I don't know how it happened; it just happened." Can you believe that? It might sound funny to you, but a lot of times that's what our lives are like. We try to figure out how we ended up harvesting something that was not good for us, even though this is exactly what we had planted. So my encouragement to you is to examine your garden right now. If you have planted a lot of weeds in your garden, get rid of them! Plant the seeds for fruit you want to produce. Choose the fruit of generosity, kindness and goodness, of hope, of vision, of goal setting, of believing the impossible can become possible. Plant these things. Plant only good things in your heart, and don't waste your time growing evil things in your soul. Let me assure you of this: you are going to be blessed and successful in your harvest if you plant the noble things of the kingdom of Christ. You need to believe and realize that you DO have control over what you are planting, and you thereby control your future harvest; you do have a say as to what you will reap. Also, don't get discouraged about the past if you planted a bad crop. In time, the new crop will overcome the bad decisions of the past. When people see your new life in Christ, they will tell you that you are so lucky. Just know that they are WRONG. Growing a good crop does not require luck. It requires planning, choosing right, and allowing God's spirit to nurture you. Others can call it luck, but just know that it's the truth that comes from knowing the law of sowing and reaping. It's the 'law of the farm.' What you plant is what you harvest. Remember that you can't deceive God; He knows what you are planting. Plant good things so that you can reap good things that will be a blessing to your life.

The Word of God Section

"God called the dry ground "land," and the gathered waters he called "seas." And God saw that it was good. Then God said, "Let the land produce vegetation: seed-bearing plants and trees on the land that bear fruit with seed in it, according to their various kinds." And it was so. The land produced vegetation: plants bearing seed according to their kinds and trees bearing fruit with seed in it according to their kinds. And God saw that it was good." (Genesis 1:10-12)

"Blessed is the one who does not walk in step with the wicked or stand in the way that sinners take or sit in the company of mockers, but whose delight is in the law of the LORD, and who meditates on his law day and night. That person is like a tree planted by streams of water, which yields its fruit in season and whose leaf does not wither— whatever they do prospers." (Psalm 1:1-3)

"Whoever brings ruin on their family will inherit only wind, and the fool will be servant to the wise. The fruit of the righteous is a tree of life, and the one who is wise saves lives. If the righteous receive their due on earth, how much more the ungodly and the sinner!" (Proverbs 11:29-31)

"The look on their faces testifies against them; they parade their sin like Sodom; they do not hide it. Woe to them! They have brought disaster upon themselves. Tell the righteous it will be well with them, for they will enjoy the fruit of their deeds. Woe to the wicked! Disaster is upon them! They will be paid back for what their hands have done." (Isaiah 3:9-11)

"But blessed is the one who trusts in the LORD, whose confidence is in him. They will be like a tree planted by the water that sends out its roots by the stream. It does not fear when heat comes; its leaves are always green. It has no worries in a year of drought and never fails to bear fruit." (Jeremiah 17:7-8)

"Remain in me, as I also remain in you. No branch can bear fruit by itself; it must remain in the vine. Neither can you bear fruit unless you remain in me. "I am the vine; you are the branches. If you remain in me and I in you, you will bear much fruit; apart from me you can do nothing." (John 15:4-5)

"The acts of the flesh are obvious: sexual immorality, impurity and debauchery; idolatry and witchcraft; hatred, discord, jealousy, fits of rage, selfish ambition, dissensions, factions and envy; drunkenness, orgies, and the like. I warn you, as I did before, that those who live like this will not inherit the kingdom of God. But the fruit of the Spirit is love, joy, peace, forbearance, kindness, goodness, faithfulness, gentleness and self-control. Against such things there is no law." (Galatians 5:19-23)

Successful Living
30 Powerful Biblical Truths
(1-5)

Volume 1 of 6

Marco A. Martinez
www.30biblicaltruths.com

Made in the USA
Charleston, SC
22 June 2014